Dear Daughter

Letters from Eve and Other Women of the Bible

by
Colleen Ivey Hartsoe

Morehouse-Barlow Co., Inc.
Wilton, Connecticut

Dedicated to
The Women of St. Mary's Episcopal Church
High Point, North Carolina

Morehouse-Barlow Co., Inc.
78 Danbury Road
Wilton, Connecticut 06897

ISBN 0-8192-1288-1

Library of Congress Catalog Card Number 81-80627

Printed in the United States of America

Table of Contents

Preface

This book came about as a result of a series of programs I prepared for a Churchwomen's group. My goal was to take a new look at the women in the Bible: 1) to see what was literally there in the pages, 2) to see how the prejudice of the men writers entered into the original account, and 3) to suggest that current church practices may be based on this same sort of prejudice.

Feminist theologians would say this has already been done, I find, however, that these concepts are still not widespread for most women in the pew, often because the validity of the Bible seems threatened.

I am writing for the woman who studies the Scriptures and believes the Holy Spirit continues to speak through its pages.

I want to acknowledge the help and encouragement of my husband, Charles, and of my friend, Betty McDonald, who also typed the manuscript.

C. I. H.

Introduction

Bible students are thrilled when archaeologists make new discoveries, especially of written records such as the Dead Sea Scrolls. There is one group of people whose personal records will never be found because they were never written.

The women of the Bible are there in its pages. Although the men writers were biased by the patriarchal culture of the times, they still preserved for us stories that are rich in explicit and implicit details about the women characters.

I believe women as well as men were trying to find answers to theological questions: Where did I come from? Why am I here? Is there a God that cares about me? What does God want from me? Why is there evil in the world? Does the end justify the means? Yet, the ultimate meanings these women were thinking about have been generally ignored by Judaeo-Christian tradition.

I have tried to imagine what this thinking might have been. These are the letters the women might have written, letters to all women even today. I have followed statements and suggestions I found in the Bible itself: the New English Bible and on rare occasion the King James. Because of this, I invite the reader to review the actual Scripture before reading the letter based on it. So many of us think we know a familiar Bible story by heart only to discover after close reading that what we really knew was an altered version handed down to us through the earliest bards and scribes, then painters, poets, and clergymen.

I, of course, have a point of view, and it is that Jesus of Nazareth comprehended completely that both woman and man were created in the image of God. He left it to his church to apply this concept to daily life. Sadly, however, even before the death of Paul, the church began to falter in its obligation to treat women as equals to men.

One

Letter from Eve

Based on Genesis 2:5-5:5 (New English Bible)

Date: unknown

> The Lord God made trees spring from the ground, all trees pleasant to look at and good for food; and in the middle of the garden he set the tree of life and the tree of the knowledge of good and evil.
>
> Genesis 2:9

> The Lord God took the man and put him in the garden of Eden to till it and care for it. He told the man, 'You may eat from every tree in the garden, but not from the tree of the knowledge of good and evil; for on the day that you eat from it, you will certainly die.' Then the Lord God said, 'It is not good for the man to be alone. I will provide a partner for him.'
>
> Genesis 2:15-18

Dear Daughter,

As I grow older, I look back at my life in search of meaning that will survive me. Through the years your father, Adam, has related much family history to your brothers. Already in my lifetime songs are being sung around our homefires about Cain and Seth and their children. No one has made a song about you; for generations to come you will remain nameless. But, beloved Daughter-Without-A-Name, there is something about me that I want you to know. It concerns a time when I felt very close to God and to truth.

You have heard your father tell of the beautiful home in Eden he and I shared many years ago. I remember clearly the tree whose fruit Adam told me God did not want us to eat.

"Why?" I asked.

"It is the tree of the knowledge of good and evil," he told me, "and if we eat of it we will die."

"But Adam," I puzzled, "surely to be human as God means us to be, we must learn to know good from evil. We cannot avoid eating this fruit even if it does mean death. What can our lives mean if we have no standards to live by?"

Adam chastised me saying we had plenty to eat and drink; we were comfortable; we had no hard decisions to make.

I worried about the quality of our lives. As I knelt in prayer, I felt certain God meant for us to make a decision, take this step toward complete humanity and strive to know good from evil. I believed it was Satan who wanted us to stay in ignorance. Finally I convinced Adam I was right, although he argued, "Then why did God tell me we were not to eat this fruit?"

I answered, "But Adam, you told me he said *if* we ate it, we would die. He was giving us a choice to make. He was honest and told you to know good is also to know death."

So we ate, both of us.

And our eyes were indeed opened. We saw famine in the sun's drying a blade of grass; we saw havoc of storms in a gentle breeze's spinning in a spiral. An eagle dipped down and captured a small rabbit and we knew animal cruelty. We looked at one another and we saw not perfection but frailty. We recognized our sexuality as a potential for creation or destruction.

We saw the burden of decision making. We understood responsibility. We reached out to each other for comfort, for love.

Then God spoke. We hid from him because we felt so unworthy of his gifts and of the terrible humanity we had chosen. My voice caught in my throat but Adam answered.

"I am afraid, God. I stand naked, bared before you in my weakness."

God's voice was kind. "You have chosen to know good from evil, Adam, Eve. Now you will know death. How can I teach you that only from death comes life?"

And God did not desert us, but clothed us in garments he sewed with his own hands.

God's words about life's coming from death remained a riddle. We made decisions that seemed good to us. We saw some plants and animals as good and others as evil. We invented the word "weather" for now we called even that aspect of nature good or bad. We saw problems and we worked on solutions and there was a new kind of happiness when we succeeded but also a new despair when we failed.

Then came the long night when I labored to give birth to our first child, your brother Cain. I was in great pain and Adam cried out against God. Adam suffered because I suffered and because he felt responsible.

"All this suffering cannot be part of God's will," Adam said. "You believed God meant for us to know good from evil, but you were wrong. It was surely Satan who spoke to you when you were praying."

And Adam wept.

I knew he was wrong. I knew that he spoke out of his fears for me and the child in the world we now knew. He could not face the fact that we cause suffering to each other.

Many times I heard him repeat to your brothers and to you his story of our perfect garden and our misunderstanding of God's will.

Then came the day of our greatest sorrow, the sorrow that never leaves us. Our firstborn came to us confessing he had murdered his brother. Two sons lost, and if grief can be measured, my heart broke the deeper for Cain. I could accept even this as one of the consequences of living as a free human being. Your father could only cry out to God for reasons. From then on he began to tell himself I was more to blame than he. He saw my pain in childbirth as a special punishment for me. The story told to our grand-children finally became a story of my fall and my leading Adam to sin.

Why was I silent? Looking back I see that I came to believe what he said. Life was full of evil. It was hard to maintain the conviction that evil was created by our own choices. Adam's belief was not so difficult for me to go along with. He loved me, he saw me as weak and yet as mysteriously desirable. His arms were a refuge. God seemed far away.

I had to tell you the truth. In my old age I see my earliest experiences so much more clearly. Beloved daughter, what lies ahead for you? A myth is hard to change.

I sign this your loving mother,

Eve

Two

Letter from Sarah to her sister-in-law

Based on Genesis 11:27-13:18; 15:1-5; 16; 17; 18; 21; 22 (NEB)

Date: 1800-1550 B.C.

> After this the word of the Lord came to Abram in a vision. He said, 'Do not be afraid, Abram, I am giving you a very great reward.' Abram replied, 'Lord God, what canst thou give me? I have no standing among men, for the heir to my household is Eliezer of Damascus.' Abram continued, 'Thou hast given me no children, and so my heir must be a slave born in my house.'
>
> Genesis 15:1-3

Dear Milcah,

From the day you married Abraham's brother Nahor you have been as a sister to me. Often I have longed to talk to you. Papyrus is scarce and so is a servant who can write. Abraham's loyal Eliezer has always been a friend to me and he agreed to write this letter in confidence.

Word has come to us that at last you have a granddaughter. Abraham has always been envious of the eight sons you bore to Nahor, but I knew you wished in vain for one daughter. I hope this grandchild, Rebecca, will bring joy to you. So

10

now you are a grandmother while I have only been a mother for a few years! Isaac is a wonderful little boy; I wish you could see him. When I heard of the birth of Rebecca, the idea of a betrothal between the two crossed my mind. When the time is right, I may mention it to Abraham; it is not easy to get him to take advice concerning Isaac. I am not young and my health is failing. I want it recorded that I would approve a marriage between Isaac and Rebecca. Sometimes one's wish, ignored in life, has more effect from the grave. If your granddaughter should become my daughter-in-law, give her this letter so she may know something of me as well as of Abraham.

It has not been easy to be the wife of a man who has visions and feels God speaks clearly and directly to him. Abraham has never questioned his understanding of God's will. I confess I have had many doubts through the years.

When Abraham told me God had called him to leave our home and family and go to an unknown land, I was frightened and in despair. In my heart I felt your brother Lot had influenced Abraham to make the move. I had no children to fill my life; your sons were like my own. How could I leave all of you? But even had I had a choice, I would have gone with Abraham. I had always known my husband believed himself a poor man in spite of his wealth in cattle and gold, a poor man because I failed to give him a child. Yet, he had taken no other woman and I loved him for this. Having no sons to carry on his name, Abraham was eager to believe what he had heard God say, ". . . I will make your name so great that it shall be used in blessings . . . all the families on earth will pray to be blessed as you are blessed" (Genesis 12:2-3).

We lived as simple herdsmen moving from place to place. Famine struck us and we went into Egypt to live for awhile. Lonely and afraid, I was called on by Abraham to show my love for him in a difficult way. Because I was young and beautiful, Abraham hoped I would be taken to Pharaoh's harem. "Tell them you are my sister, so that all may go well with me," he said. I entered the harem and Abraham did indeed receive sheep, cattle, camels, and male and female slaves. So wealth came to him again, bought with my body. For the first time I was glad I was barren, for I knew I would not bear another man's child.

Grave illness fell on Pharaoh's household. I wondered who had the courage to suggest to Pharaoh that the illness came because the wife of Abraham lived in a harem chamber. Secretly I have always suspected Eliezer, who does not deny it as I dictate this letter to him.

I was released. We left Egypt and began our wandering again. I was pleased when Lot and his family separated from us. Abraham and I were starting over together.

Then Abraham came to me and told me God had spoken to him again saying, "I will make your descendants countless as the dust of the earth" (Genesis 13:16). I knew Abraham believed this; his face shone with the hope of fathering children. My barrenness was still his greatest disappointment; nothing had changed. How could I hold on to his love? In desperation I did what had been done to me. As I was given in adultery to Pharaoh, so I took my young slave-girl Hagar and gave her to Abraham. Hagar belonged to me; legally her child would belong to me. However, laws do not make a truth. Hagar's pregnancy and Abraham's joy in it were painful to me. I hated her. I hated myself. I wanted to die. Believing Hagar held me in contempt because of my empty womb, I treated her cruelly. Once she ran away but returned saying God had spoken to her! So, God spoke to my husband and to his concubine, but not to me. Abraham's son Ishmael was born and they shared great happiness. I was indeed alone.

It was years later that I began to have symptoms of pregnancy. I felt God was mocking me. Hiding my grief, I went to Abraham. I laughed and tried to make a joke. "An old woman like me, with an old husband, thinking she is pregnant! Surely I am a little crazy!" Abraham turned from me and went into his tent to pray. When he came out he announced that God had once again spoken to him saying, "I will bless Sarah and give you a son by her. You shall call the boy Isaac. With him I will fulfill my covenant." Mirthlessly I laughed again. We are all crazy I thought and we live in an absurd world. But, God had indeed performed a miracle. In my old age I delivered a son.

Abraham knew the danger of two sons both claiming to be the heir to a great religious movement. He decided to banish Hagar and Ishmael. He told his followers that God had spoken to him saying that this was the right thing to do. I honestly admit I wanted Hagar and Ishmael out of our lives. For once I was glad God spoke to Abraham directly.

This was a bad time for Abraham. He could not banish his love for Ishmael. One child cannot replace another. He looked at Isaac and saw another little boy whose eyes had shown disbelief that his father could send him away. Abraham brooded and prayed night and day; I feared for his sanity.

I shall never forget the horror when Abraham came to me with God's latest message to him. "Take your son Isaac, your only son, whom you love. You shall offer him as a sacrifice on one of the hills of Moriah" (Genesis 22:2-3).

I screamed, I wept, I said words I had not dared to utter before.

> You told me it was God's will I should leave my home and my family. You told me it was God's will I should go to the bed of Pharaoh. You told me it was God's will that you have a son and I humiliated myself and a young slave-girl that Ishmael might be conceived. And now you tell me it is God's will our son must die? Abraham, Abraham, it is your own guilt speaking to you. Because you sent Ishmael into the

wilderness you think giving up Isaac will atone for your sin.
I do not know the God that speaks to you, Abraham. I know
a God who rescued me from Pharaoh's harem, a God who
gave me a son in my old age, a God who kept Hagar and
Ishmael safe even as you and I sinned against them. That is
the God whom I worship.

Torn apart with fear, I fell to the floor. Abraham was silent
as he lifted the flap of the tent opening and strode out. I got
to my feet and followed. I saw him load the firewood onto
the ass's back; I saw him take Isaac's small hand. Leading
the child and the pack animal, he walked slowly away toward
the hills of Moriah.

Evening came. I lay exhausted and tearless on my bed.
Then I heard the voices of Abraham and Isaac and thought
my imagination tricked me. The prayer I had not dared to
pray had been answered. Abraham came to me and told me
God had once more spoken to him. As was his way, Abraham's own voice was full of confidence as he repeated to me
what had happened. " As I lifted the knife to slay Isaac, I
heard God's voice telling me I had already proved my faith!"

I held my child in my arms and I thanked God for staying
the hand of Abraham. It seemed to me that at last I heard
the voice of God speaking to me, Sarah, saying, "Sarah, I
did speak to Abraham today, but not there on the hill. It
was through you I spoke. You knew I could not want a small
boy as a burnt offering. It is you that have understood sin,
forgiveness, and love." I was at peace, forgiven, redeemed.

I did not tell Abraham God had spoken to me. Only you,
Milcah, shall know, and dear Eliezer, whose eyes are so full
of tears he can write no more.

Your sister,

Sarah

Three

Letter from Rebecca to Milcah

Based on Genesis 24:1-67; 25; 26; 27; 28:1-9 (NEB)

Date: 1800-1550 B.C.

As Sarah had hoped, Rebecca and Isaac did marry. Their children were Esau and Jacob. As Rebecca's son Jacob is sent out to find a wife, Rebecca recalls her own engagement and marriage to Isaac.

Dear Grandmother,

My son Jacob is leaving at dawn tomorrow to make the long trip to Paddan-aram. He brings a letter from my husband Isaac to my brother Laban asking for one of Laban's daughters in marriage. The opportunity to write to you gives me much pleasure. It was so many years ago that I left home to come to Canaan and marry Isaac. I still remember all you told me about Abraham and Sarah.

Even as a little girl I had heard of Abraham, a man not only wealthy and powerful but a great leader destined by God to create a nation. I wished I could be the wife of a man such as he! I imagined myself mighty as any Philistine queen, sharing glory with my husband! I believed my dream had come true when I was married to Isaac, son of Abraham.

Do you remember how it all began? More than twenty years ago, I, a romantic young girl aware of my own beauty and ambition, went to the village well to draw water and

found my destiny instead. There I met the mysterious caravan leader who requested a drink of water. Of course I
obliged him and even stayed to water his camels! Nothing
could have pulled me away. My mind danced with images
of what wonderful things might be hidden in the heavy
bundles the camels carried. The old man who spoke to me
gave me gold bracelets and rings, more beautiful than any I
had seen. Boldly I told him my family's name and invited
him to our house for the night.

He bowed to the ground and prayed aloud to the Lord
puzzling words about being blessed and guided to our home.
I ran home and showed my brother Laban my gifts and told
him about the stranger's prayer. Laban then rushed to the
well, found the man, and asked his whole caravan to stay
with our family.

Food and drink were set out but the man would not eat
until he told us why he was there. What an exciting story it
was! And, I, Rebecca, was the main character! He said it
was an angel from God who led me to offer him a drink at
the well. He said I was the woman he wanted as wife for the
son of Abraham. I still hear the words he used to describe
Abraham. "He has become a man of power. The Lord has
given him flocks and herds, silver and gold, male and female
slaves, camels and asses" (Genesis 24:35).

My father and brother agreed immediately to the match.
What gifts appeared then: gold and silver ornaments, robes
for me, my mother, as well as for Laban and my father.

The servant of Abraham wanted to leave the next morning.
My family begged that he give us a few more days together.
Do you remember how they called me and asked if I were
willing to go so soon? Dazzled with visions of my newfound
wealth, I was eager to move on to meet my husband.

I learned soon enough that Isaac was not the man his
father was. Abraham, though old, was still virile. He wielded
power as a great man should. I never tired of hearing him

tell how God had chosen him to create a nation, and how his son Isaac was the heir to this kingly role.

Would that I had been wife to such a man as Abraham! But my husband was Isaac, a man more in the image of his mother Sarah. On our wedding day Isaac told me how Sarah had died when he was a young boy, how close they had been, how lonely his days were without her. He told me about the time his father placed him on an altar of rocks, held a knife to his heart, and offered to sacrifice his life to God. "But Isaac," I reasoned, "Abraham made you his first heir; he must love you."

"No," replied Isaac, "my father believes it is God's will I succeed him, and so he has made me his heir, but it is my brother Ishmael he admires and loves."

At the time of Abraham's death, Isaac and I had no children. Abraham had many other sons. There was Ishmael, always a threat to Isaac's position, who himself had twelve sons, and there were six more sons born to Abraham's second wife Keturah. Concubines had also produced male offspring to Abraham. After the property was divided, Isaac and I were no longer wealthy, but I believed all that Abraham had told me about God's will for his line through Isaac.

At last I conceived. It was a difficult pregnancy. I gave birth to twin sons, Esau and Jacob. Because Esau was a few minutes older, he was considered the firstborn. He was never first in my heart however. He was unattractive, covered with heavy hair, dull of wit, and skillful only at hunting. I could not imagine Esau's carrying out the prophecy God had made for Abraham's family. If we were to regain our power and wealth, it must be through Jacob.

I kept Jacob with me among the tents. I filled his mind with stories of our family; especially I talked to him about his grandfather Abraham. I told him that even during my pregnancy he and Esau had seemed to struggle with each other. I confided that God had actually spoken to me, as he used to speak to Abraham, saying my older son should be servant to the younger.

One day Esau came in tired and hungry from hunting. Jacob had just prepared a delicious smelling broth. When Esau asked for some to drink, Jacob replied, "Not until you sell me your rights as firstborn!" Esau showed how little he valued his birthright because he easily gave in to Jacob's demand.

Soon after this the family fortune began to improve. Isaac became almost as wealthy as Abraham had been. I took this as sign that God approved of my ambition for Jacob. Esau again demonstrated his lack of understanding of our family's position when he took two Hittite women as wives. Even Isaac grieved bitterly over this, but his affection for Esau was unchanged. I believe Isaac considered Esau more manly than Jacob. He admired Esau's physical strength and his hunting skills. He often accused me of keeping Jacob too close to me.

Isaac grew old and became blind. He began to think about death and settling his affairs. One day when he felt particularly ill, he called Esau to him saying, "I am about to die; just one more time go out into the country and get me some venison to eat. When I have eaten, then I will give you my blessing." Of course Esau took his hunting gear and went off into the deer country.

I decided if Isaac's blessing was to be bought with a tasty dish, perhaps I could help Jacob secure it. I recalled how Abraham, whom I admired so much, had turned aside from his firstborn Ishmael and passed the role of family leader to Isaac. I would be doing no more than he had done. I too would carry out God's will as revealed to me! So I planned with Jacob how to trick his father.

Dressed in Esau's clothes, with hairy goatskins on his neck and hands, with a dish of savoury stew made from two young goats, Jacob came close to his father. Isaac was deceived, and he gave the blessing, "Peoples shall serve you. Nations bow down to you. Be lord over your brother" (Genesis 27:29).

When Esau returned from hunting and found out what had happened, he was very angry. He told everyone he planned to kill Jacob. I knew he would do nothing while his father yet lived; so I had time to get Jacob away from home. I went to Isaac and said, "I am weary to death of Hittite women. If Jacob marries a Hittite woman, my life will not be worth living" (Genesis 27:46).

Isaac called Jacob to him and gave him instructions, "Go at once to Paddan-aram, and there find a wife, one of the daughters of Laban, your mother's brother" (Genesis 28:2-3).

So, Grandmother, it would seem that my dreams have come true. The son I chose has become heir to Abraham and Isaac and he will soon have a wife from our people.

I sign this letter,

Rebecca
Handmaiden of the Lord

Four

Letter from Leah to her daughter

Based on Genesis 29; 30:14-26; 32; 33; 34 (NEB)

Date: 1800-1550 B.C.

> Dinah, the daughter whom Leah had borne to Jacob, went
> out to visit the women of the country, and Shechem, son of
> Hamor the Hivite, the local prince, saw her; he took her, lay
> with her and dishonored her. But he remained true to Jacob's
> daughter Dinah; he loved the girl and comforted her. So
> Shechem said to his father Hamor, 'Get me this girl for a
> wife.'
>
> Genesis 34:1-4

Dearest Dinah,

I have received news of the tragedy that has befallen you.
Your brothers Simeon and Levi have murdered the man
you had hoped to marry. What can I say to comfort you?
Your future is bleak; no Hebrew man will want you for
a wife because he will believe you were dishonored by
Shechem.

Will it help you to know I do not feel you were dishonored?
A young prince fell in love with you. With his father's
approval and offering any price, he begged for you in marriage. Did you go to his bed because he forced you or because
you loved him and hoped this act would persuade your

father and brothers to allow the marriage? No one has reported to me your feelings or your wishes. I know only that your brothers saw Shechem's love for you as an excuse to murder, plunder, and steal.

You face years of loneliness as the servant of your brothers' wives, a woman with no rights. I, who have had a husband, six sons, a daughter, slave-girls to serve me, fine tents, golden bracelets, I, your mother, have never known the love you had so briefly. In your grief can you believe I envy you?

I was forced into the bed of Jacob who never loved me. Because it was my father who put me there, was my honor intact while yours was destroyed? The men of our family used me, and now you, for their own purposes.

Daughter, I cannot dry your tears but I can share my own sad story with you. "Dull-eyed Leah" . . . did you know this was how my own father described me? A daughter's only value was to attract a well-to-do husband and I always knew I was worthless. How I envied my beautiful younger sister Rachel. Can you imagine how it was growing up beside her, constantly aware of my homeliness, knowing I was a disappointment to my family?

When my cousin Jacob came out of the land of Canaan looking for a wife, he saw Rachel and at once wanted her. My father demanded seven years indenture from Jacob in return for Rachel. During all those years I knew Jacob dreamed of the day he would marry Rachel. And during those years no man asked for me. On the eve of the wedding my father saw his chance to get rid of me. After Jacob had eaten and drunk much and had fallen asleep, I was ordered to go into his tent and lie down beside him.

When Jacob found me on his couch the next morning, he knew he had been tricked. The wedding festivities that followed celebrated his marriage to me, not to Rachel. Jacob agreed to work another seven years for my father if he could also have Rachel as wife. I knew how he must love her and how he must despise me.

I prayed I could find some favor in my husband's eyes. I bore him four sons and believed this would make him love me. I was wrong. Even though Rachel could not conceive a child, Jacob still preferred her over me.

For a few years I had no more children and Jacob turned away from me. I sent my son Reuben into the country to find mandrake roots from which I made a fertility potion. But of what worth to drink such a potion if Jacob scorned my bed? So I humbled myself and went to Rachel. I offered her half my magical mandrakes if she would persuade Jacob to sleep one night with me.

Because my sister was desperate herself, the plan succeeded and in time I bore Jacob two more sons and then you, my daughter Dinah. I was certain Jacob would treat me as his favorite wife. In vain I hoped.

The potion of mandrakes had not worked for Rachel but God at last heard her prayer and she delivered her first child, a son named Joseph.

Only after Joseph was born did Jacob go to my father Laban and make arrangements to return to his own land of Canaan. It was clear to me that it was the birth of Joseph that made Jacob feel he had a true heir to the line of Abraham and Isaac. Now he was willing to go home, confront his brother Esau, and perhaps face a struggle for tribal leadership.

My humiliation was not yet complete. Fearful that Esau would meet him with armed men, Jacob arranged his company in the order he considered them expendable. He sent on ahead servants and animals. Then came the family: first his concubines and their children, then I and my children, and last Rachel and her son Joseph.

No sacrifice of life was needed however. Much to my astonishment Esau was kind and greeted us graciously. In the glow of many evening campfires I had heard Jacob tell how his brother hated him. Esau did not act like a man who hated. He was a simple, artless person with a good heart. He had put the trickery of his mother and brother behind him. Even so, it is apparent now that Jacob and Esau will not long share land. Jacob continues to believe he has been chosen by God to found a nation called Israel. I will miss Esau and his wives when we again separate. It has been a brief pleasure to spend time with people who do not think of me as "dull-eyed Leah".

We women were created by the Lord God. In our creation surely we were given a kind of honor that cannot be taken from us at the whim of men. If your brothers allow you to come home, Dinah, I cannot promise you a relief from loneliness, but I will love you always.

Your mother,

Leah

Five

Letter from Jael to her fellow revolutionary

Based on Judges 4 and 5 (NEB)

Date: 1100-1000 B.C.

> The Israelites cried to the Lord for help, because Sisera had nine hundred chariots of iron and had oppressed Israel harshly for twenty years. At that time Deborah wife of Lappidoth, a prophetess, was judge in Israel. . . . She sent for Barak . . . and said to him, 'These are the commands of the Lord the God of Israel: . . .'
>
> Judges 4:3-6

Dear Deborah,

Many years ago on this day God gave victory to the Israelites over Jabin king of Canaan and his commander Sisera. What a glorious day it was! You and Barak, leader of our fighting force, led a triumphant procession. How the people cheered! The two of you sang a great song of victory. I especially remember the words you sang about me:

> Blest above women be Jael,
> The wife of Heber the Kenite
> Blest above all women in the tents.
>
> Judges 5:24

I sit here alone remembering that day when I felt the equal of any brave Israelite, man or woman. The words of your song ring in my ears, and yet as I consider the years that followed, I ask myself why does everyone know the name of Deborah the judge but few remember me? People name their daughters Deborah; no one honors my name in such a fashion.

The whole military operation was your idea. You sent for Barak. You told him God had commanded him to amass ten thousand men and face the Canaanite commander Sisera with his men and their nine hundred chariots in the valley beneath Mount Tabor. You even marched beside Barak. Such a marvelous sight that must have been for our Israelite daughters to see . . . a man and a woman together leading the army!

I did not see it but heard about it in my husband's tent. Heber was sad as he told me about the battle, sad because his lord, the king of Canaan, had seen his great commander Sisera defeated that day. The whole Canaanite army was put to the sword. Only Sisera himself escaped on foot.

Alone in the tent the next day I was caught up in my dreams of being part of a group of people who let men and women lead together. As if hearing my prayer, the Lord delivered Sisera into my hands!

There at my tent door he stood, looking for food and drink. He was exhausted from running. He lay back on a pile of hides in the corner of the tent. After I gave him milk to drink, he fell asleep and I covered him up.

Both my husband and I are descendants of the brother-in-law of Moses. Heber had never told me why we had left our people and pitched our tent in the domain of King Jabin. I have never been able to forget the stories I heard as a child about my people.

The true Israelite would do anything to preserve his people and to fulfill the word of God. I remembered that Abraham had sent Hagar and her child into the wilderness to starve. He had even been ready to sacrifice the life of Isaac.

Even Jacob was a deceitful man, but all to the glory of God.

I remembered the many stories of the prophet Joshua. He committed violence in the name of God. I hear the words of the ballad singer still ringing in my ears:

> Joshua and his forces captured the city and put its king to death with the sword. They killed every living thing in it and wiped them all out; they spared nothing that drew breath.
>
> Joshua 11:10-11

And there was the great Moses who killed the cruel Egyptian overseer and hid his body in the sand.

Aglow with memories of these revered men, ignoring my husband's politics, I determined to do my part as a daughter of Israel.

I took up a tent-peg and a hammer and crept up to Sisera as he slept. I drove the peg into his skull and he died. When Barak came in pursuit of Sisera, I went out to meet him and said to him, "Come, I will show you the man you are looking for."

That was the day you, Deborah, and Barak sang your song of praise and called me blest above all women in the tents. If that is so, why is my name hardly mentioned in the histories men write? Surely it was not wrong to murder in the name of God; our great heroes did no less. What was the difference between you and me, Deborah? You had the idea of multiple murder in battle; I only killed one man. Was it because I, a woman, made a decision of which my husband would not have approved and acted on this decision? Was my sin against my husband greater than my contribution to the cause of our people?

I am confused, Deborah. You are a clever woman, a judge, a prophet. Can you tell me why no girl children are named for me?

I sign this,

Jael the Lonely

Six

Letter from Delilah to Samson's mother

Based on Judges 13; 14; 15; 16 (NEB)

Date: 1100-1000 B.C.

> The woman went and told her husband; she said to him, 'A man of God came to me; his appearance was that of an angel of God, most terrible to see. I did not ask him where he came from nor did he tell me his name. He said to me, "You shall conceive and give birth to a son. . . . the boy is to be a Nazirite consecrated to God . . ."'
>
> Judges 13:6-7

To the wife of Manoah,

I do not know your name, madam. It has not been spread across the country in ignominy as has mine. I am sick to death of the stories your family has told about me. I am making this statement about your son Samson. Perhaps some Israelite singer will tell the whole truth of his downfall.

While Samson was a judge of Israel, he fell in love with me, a woman not of his religion nor of his country. I knew how the Israelites felt about such relationships. So I was sure he did not have marriage in mind. How could a Hebrew judge consider marriage with me, a woman of Sorek? Be that as it may, I certainly would not have wanted to marry him. At best marriage was benign bondage for a woman and

it would have been hell with a man whose temper was
uncontrollable. Samson offered an opportunity to get some
money of my own, to acquire some independence. I am an
honest woman. I did not deceive your son; he deceived
himself.

You are the woman who was never honest with him. From
the day he was born you filled his head with ideas of gran-
deur. You convinced him he had a special mission from
God to strike a blow against the Philistines. Whenever he
lost his temper, you told him, and yourself, that the spirit of
the Lord had come over him. You gave in to his wishes,
even agreed to his marriage with a Philistine woman.

Your son was stupid. He took a silly riddle as seriously as
he did a matter of life and death. Because his wife told the
answer to his riddle, he murdered thirty men! Was that the
action of a man consecrated to your God?

In his anger Samson left his wife and returned home to
you. Deserted by her groom, the bride was given in marriage
to another man. Later, when Samson changed his mind,
decided to go back to claim a husband's rights, he was
angered to find she was no longer his. As was to be expected,
his temper flared uncontrollably and he burned all the corn-
fields of the Philistines.

After this he lived wifeless in a cave. However, do not
think he was rejecting the flesh; he thought nothing of
visiting a prostitute in Gaza! Were you proud of your son,
dedicated since birth to your Hebrew God?

It was at this point in his life that his eye fell on me. I did
not want the attention of such a wild man, a man of super-
human strength with a bad temper. But how was I to rid
myself of him? I was fortunate that the Philistines also
wanted him out of the way. When they came and offered
me eleven hundred pieces of silver to help them, I was
elated. The story has been told of my betrayal of Samson.
Can a person betray an enemy?

You are the woman who betrayed your son. You convinced him he could safely do whatever he desired. It is true you warned him his strength would disappear if he cut his hair but he did not believe you.

It is impossible that he believed you. Three times I repeated what he had told me to the Philistines and yet he trusted me a fourth time. Ridiculous, even for a stupid man! He simply could not imagine that his strength would ever leave him. Even when he found his hair had been cut, he expected to break his bonds.

So at the end your son had his moment of greatness. It is true he sacrificed his own life in order to kill many Philistines. I take no credit for that moment, as I take no blame for the events that led him into captivity. Look into your own heart, wife of Manoah, if you must have reasons.

Signed,

Delilah, wife of no man

Seven

Letter from Ruth to her sister-in-law

Based on The Book of Ruth (NEB)

Date: 1100-1000 B.C.

> Long ago, in the time of the Judges, there was a famine in
> the land, and a man from Bethlehem in Judah went to live in
> the Moabite country with his wife and his two sons. The
> man's name was Elimelech, his wife's name was Naomi, and
> the names of his two sons Mahlon and Chilion. . . .
>
> Ruth 1:1-2

Dear Orpah,

It is the harvest time here in Judah. I sit looking out at the
fields of grain and watching the reapers at work. My husband Boaz is wealthy and I do not have to help in the harvest.
In fact, I do not have much of anything to do. Even my
little boy is being cared for by Naomi. I am lonely, Orpah,
and I have no one with whom to share my feelings. Often I
wonder how things have gone for you.

Both of us were very young when we married Naomi's
sons. Naomi became a mother to us. When Mahlon and
Chilion died, it did not occur to either of us to return to our
own villages. Do you remember how we piled all our belong-
ings onto the pack animals and started off to the land of
Judah? Naomi assured us there would be no more hunger

there. We would all three face a new life together. We already knew much about the Israelite customs and about the special God they worshiped. We looked forward to living in a place where the whole community worshiped as one.

I never knew why Naomi changed her mind as we approached the border of Judah. Did she begin to think about the fate of three women in Judah with no male protector? Did she begin to feel sorry for herself, with no husband, no sons? Did she consider her own chance of re-marriage would be jeopardized if she had two foreign daughters-in-law?

I do remember the dismay and fear that crawled up my back when she stopped in the road and spoke to us, saying, "Go back, both of you, to your mothers' homes." We felt like young pups being ordered away from their master. We began to sob loudly. Naomi told us she had nothing to offer us; she chastised us for weeping and declared, "My lot is more bitter than yours, for the Lord has been against me."

Orpah, you then kissed Naomi and left to return to your people. I could not find the courage to follow your example even though Naomi pointed out to me, "You see, your sister-in-law has gone back to her people and her gods; go back with her."

Maybe without realizing it I had become a believer in the Hebrew God. I wanted a sense of purpose and direction in my life. Mahlon's family had never let me forget I was a Moabite. Maybe they had not understood how I longed for something to really belong to. I decided to confess my faith. I spoke from my deepest convictions when I said to Naomi:

> Do not urge me to go back and desert you. Where you go, I will go, and where you stay, I will stay. Your people shall be my people, and your God my God. Where you die, I will die, and there I will be buried. I swear a solemn oath before the Lord your God: nothing but death shall divide us.
>
> Ruth 1:16-18

Naomi said no more and allowed me to follow her to
Bethlehem in Judah. How excited the villagers were to see
her. "Can this be Naomi!" they exclaimed. Naomi answered
them in a strange way then:

> Do not call me Naomi; call me Bitter, for it is a bitter lot
> that the Almighty has sent me. I went away full, and the
> Lord has brought me back empty. Why do you call me
> Naomi? The Lord has pronounced against me; the Almighty
> has brought disaster on me."
>
> Ruth 1:20-21

I felt the shadow of rejection pass over me. I had given
myself in complete surrender to Naomi and to her God.
How could she say she was empty; how could she say
disaster was on her? I knew then she did not love me the
way I loved her. I wondered why she had let me come with
her.

The barley harvest was beginning when we arrived in
Bethlehem. Observing a way I might get food for Naomi
and me, I asked her if I might go out to the grainfields and
glean behind some land-owner's reapers. She gave her
permission and I joined other gleaners in the countryside
outside Bethlehem.

The owner of the field noticed me and called me to him.
In a kind voice he instructed me to continue to glean only
in his field. He also assured me none of his men would
molest me. When I asked him why he was being so generous
to me, a foreigner, he replied that he admired what I had
done for Naomi. As I did not feel I had done much for her,
I was suspicious of his motives. I bowed low before him
and said, "You have eased my mind and spoken kindly to
me; may I ask you as a favor not to treat me only as one of
your slave-girls?" (Ruth 2:13).

Walking away, he did not answer my plea. At mealtime
he called me to sit near him with the reapers and he saw to

it that I not only had all the roasted grain, bread, and wine I could eat, but I was allowed to save some to take home. He showed even more favor to me by telling his men to pull out some barley from the bundles to assure I had plenty to glean.

I was still apprehensive over what price I would have to pay for his favors, but he did not stop me from going back into the village that evening.

When Naomi saw the food I had saved for her besides all the barley I had gleaned, she knew someone must have taken a special interest in me. I told her his name was Boaz. She was elated and said that he was related to her family. I think Naomi's head was full of a plan right then, but she only told me to continue gleaning in Boaz's field.

When the harvest was over, I found out what Naomi had in mind. I was to slip into the threshing house after Boaz had fallen asleep, turn back the covers at his feet, and lie down. Naomi was gambling that Boaz was an honorable man and would recognize his duty as my kinsman. I knew the risk to my reputation but I had sworn a solemn oath to be obedient to Naomi.

It happened as Naomi hoped, but I am not sure Boaz was led by duty to a kinswoman. He seemed truly touched that I, a young woman, had offered myself to him who was so much older. It is true I did not find this old man attractive physically, but Naomi had made it clear our security depended on my marrying him. Boaz worked out all the legal details involved in marrying the widow of his relative Mahon and the wedding took place.

I thought at last I would be accepted as a real daughter to Naomi. Perhaps the Jews would stop speaking of me as Ruth the Moabite and see me as a member of their congregation. I wondered if God had the same rules about people as they did.

I remember the day my son was born. The women of Naomi's family said to her:

Blessed be the Lord today, for he has not left you without a
next-of-kin. May the dead man's name be kept alive in Israel.
The child will give you new life and cherish you in your old
age; for your daughter-in-law who loves you, who has proved
better to you than seven sons, has borne him.

Ruth 4:14-15

How happy I was! Now Naomi would love me. Now the
God of the Jews would truly be my God.

But, Orpah, I found only a greater sense of loneliness.
Naomi took my child and treated him as if she were the
mother. The other women even called him "Naomi's son."
His name, Obed, was given him by the family. Even today
it is still as if I had no part in his birth. I wonder if years
from now when family histories are being sung, will the
singer say "son of Naomi" or "son of Ruth," or will both
of us be forgotten and only the words "son of Boaz" endure?

I am still your sister-in-law,

Ruth

Eight

Letter from Michal to her older sister

Based on 1 Samuel 18:10-30; 19:1-17; 25:1-44
　　　　　 2 Samuel 3:2-5; 5; 6; 21; 22; 23 (NEB)

Date: 1000 B.C.

> In David's reign there was a famine that lasted year after
> year for three years. So David consulted the Lord, and he
> answered, 'Blood-guilt rests on Saul and on his family because
> he put the Gibeonites to death.' . . . King David summoned
> the Gibeonites, therefore, and said to them, 'What can be
> done for you? How can I make expiation, so that you may
> have cause to bless the Lord's own people?' The Gibeonites
> answered, 'Our feud with Saul and his family cannot be
> settled in silver and gold, and there is no man in Israel whose
> death would content us. . . . Hand over to us seven of that
> man's sons, and we will hurl them down to their death . . .'
> The king then took the two sons whom Rizpah daughter of
> Aiah had borne to Saul . . . and the five sons whom Merab,
> Saul's daughter, had borne to Adriel . . . the seven of them
> fell together. . . .
>
> 　　　　　　　　　　　　　　　　　　　　　2 Samuel 21:1-9

Dear Merab,

The season of the barley harvest is here. The season will
be a short one for the crops are poor. I do not know why the
Lord our God is holding back the rain, but I do know, as

our foremother Sarah knew, that the sacrifice of seven young men is not the will of the Lord. Dear Merab, I have been told of the horrible deaths of your five sons and of our two half-brothers. This was done at the order of my husband, David the king. The death of these seven ensures David's claim to the throne of Israel with no fear from the house of Saul. Yet the king says he was only obeying the Lord.

Do not take your affection from me, Merab. If I could, I would be with you and hold you in my arms. We would mourn together for your sons and for the children I never had. My life has been empty for a long time. I am captive in a palace; I am the wife of a king who never sees me. My greatest source of information about David comes from hearing the courtiers sing the songs he has written.

The current one must have been composed just since the death of your sons. David has always been able to mold public opinion with his use of words and this one is another powerful piece of poetry. But bitterness fills my heart when I hear:

> The Lord . . . is my refuge, my deliverer, who saves me from
>   violence.
> I will call on the Lord to whom all praise is due,
> and I shall be delivered from my enemies. . . .
> all his laws are before my eyes.
> I have not failed to follow his decrees.
> In his sight I was blameless
> and kept myself from wilful sin . . .
>
>   2 Samuel 22:3-4, 23-24

> 'He who rules men in justice,
> who rules in the fear of God,
> is like the light of morning at sunrise,
> a morning that is cloudless after rain
> and makes the grass sparkle from the earth.'
>
>   2 Samuel 23:3-4

So David believes God wants him to rule men in justice. When will the voice of God be heard to say rule women in justice?

I remember the time long ago when I was jealous of you because you were engaged to David. I loved him then. What a brave young hero I thought him and when he played on his harp and sang the old folk songs of our people, my heart was full. I know now that you and I were mere pawns in a deadly game poor deranged Father was playing with David. Your engagement was broken and you were given to Adriel and I was offered to David. I never paused to ask how you felt. All I could think of was my own joy.

I was happy for a few brief months. Then Father's depression came over him again and he plotted to kill David. I had to help my husband escape, although I wondered when I would see him again. I passed the lonely days and nights dreaming of our being together.

It was not long before news about David began to come back to me. It was not the news of his brave deeds that interested me. He was not a hero of a nation to me; he was my husband whom I loved. Of import to me was that he had taken three more wives soon after he left me. I could recite their names and the names of others he added: Ahinoam, Abigail, Maacah, Haggith, Abital, Eglah. My love for David died. The Lord took mercy on me and sent me another husband, Palti, who loved only me.

Then our father Saul died and his commander-in-chief Abner offered to make an agreement with David to support David's claim to the throne. One of David's demands was that I be sent to him. I knew I only represented a symbol to him. He had to prove that no one could take a wife of his away from him. My brother came to my home and forced me from Palti's arms. Dear Palti. He followed me weeping all the time till Abner ordered him to go back. I did not cry; I had no more tears. I dried up inside and my heart hardened.

I despised David. I never hated him more than that day he brought the Ark of the Lord into the city. Wearing only a linen shirt, he was leaping and capering in the parade. I considered this less a religious act and more another political maneuver. I was right because when I accused him of exposing himself in the sight of his slave-girls like an empty-headed fool, he replied, "Those girls you speak of will honor me for it!" David could take no criticism from me and that incident was the end of any communication between us.

I wonder, Merab, will there ever be a time when a man's attitude toward women as well as toward other men will be a test of his character? Many people call David a great king but if you see my dear lost husband, tell him there is one woman, wife to that great king, who longs to be again Palti's beloved.

Your sister,

Michal

Nine

Letter from Bathsheba to her granddaughter

Based on 1 Kings 4:11; 2 Samuel 11:1-27; 12:1-25 (NEB)

Date: 950 B.C.

> Then Nathan said to David, '. . . This is the word of the Lord the God of Israel to you: ". . . since you have despised me and taken the wife of Uriah the Hittite to be your own wife, your family shall never again have rest from the sword." . . .'
>
> 2 Samuel 12:7-10

Dear Taphath,

I spend a great deal of my time thinking of the past. When I hear the street preachers shouting out the story of David and Bathsheba, I wonder if this is how I will be remembered. Once, a long time ago, I was asked for my account but over the years most of what I said has disappeared. While my mind is still clear, I want to tell it one more time to you, my dear granddaughter.

Nathan the prophet who tells this story uses less than one hundred words to relate the incident that led to my pregnancy. His terse words are etched in my heart:

> One evening David got up from his couch and, as he walked about on the roof of the palace, he saw from there a woman bathing, and she was very beautiful. He sent to inquire who she was, and the answer came, 'It must be Bathsheba daughter of Eliam and wife of Uriah the Hittite.' So he sent messengers to fetch her, and when she came to him, he had intercourse with her, though she was still being purified after her period, and then she went home. She conceived, and sent word to David that she was pregnant.
>
> 2 Samuel 11:2-4

All these lines are true. But between them lies further truth. First, you and I know that there was nothing wrong in my discreet washing of myself on my rooftop where the rainwater was collected. Even Nathan does not accuse me of flaunting myself indecently. It was a warm evening and my mind was on my husband Uriah who was away at war.

I remember how the prophet Samuel warned our people of the danger of crowning ourselves a king. Perhaps the prophet knew a king would only have to say, "Who is that woman; bring her to me," and his will would be done. I knew I could not refuse David. My only hope lay in his reputation as a Jew who honored the Law; so I told him I was still unclean. Only I knew this; so it is one part of my account still left in the story. Law and morality and my pleading did not sway King David. He satisfied his desire for me and sent me home. I felt like a common prostitute.

When I realized I was pregnant, I was distraught. Uriah had been away too long for the child to be his. I sent word to the king. David was mindful of public opinion and I am sure he did not want his soldiers to hear that he had seduced the wife of a war hero and left her in disgrace. His own messengers were witnesses to the fact that not only was I ordered to go to the king, but he did not even know my name before that fateful night. My reputation as a virtuous woman must have helped me. Even the king dared not accuse some other man of being my lover.

David did not answer my message. I waited anxiously. A few nights later a man came to my door carrying a tray of food and wine which he said the king wanted delivered to my husband and me. I was puzzled. "Uriah is not here," I said. "He is at the battlefront." "Oh no," responded the servant, "Uriah has just left the palace after an audience with the king."

That was how I found out Uriah had been summoned by David. I realized what David's plan was. I waited all night hoping Uriah would come to me. That was also the night I found out how little Uriah loved me. He made his bed at the palace gates with the king's slaves. This symbolic act was supposed to demonstrate his commitment to his men. I later learned that on the next night David invited Uriah to eat and drink with him. Evidently my husband's loyalty to his men did not require he eat only camp rations while he was on leave, nor did he turn down the wine goblet. But even drunk, Uriah resisted any longings he had for me.

You know what happened next. David ordered Uriah to the frontlines and he was killed. I went through the mourning ritual expected of me, but in my heart I did not mourn. My tears for a husband lost had been shed the night he slept at the palace gate.

The second time I was ever in the king's presence was when he sent for me and made me one of his wives. I suppose there were those who praised David for becoming the protector and husband of the widow of a fallen hero. My only feeling was relief that my child would be born with a father's name.

My baby was delivered and for a few years I had someone to love who also loved me. It was not to last.

The prophet Nathan came to David and accused him of sin. How I loathe that sentimental parable Nathan made

famous, the story of the rich man who stole the poor man's
one little ewe lamb. I hated the idea that I was only a piece
of property. It was a tragic twist of fate to know that I was
such a valuable piece of property that Nathan prophesied
the Lord God would strike down my son because of David's
thievery.

It is true my child became very ill and died. I cannot
believe it was the will of God. I am a kinswoman to Sarah
long ago who knew her son was not meant to be a sacrifice,
and to Eve who knew life held good and evil for all people.

There is something else I know, Taphath. King David's
great sin was not that he stole Uriah's lamb. Because I,
Bathsheba, was used as an object, it was *my humanity* that
was stolen. I was never a person in the eyes of David or
Nathan; even to Uriah I was of less value than his comrades-
in-arms.

I pray that someday our Lord will raise up a prophet who
will open men's eyes and they will see that from the very
beginning of time all the little ewe lambs were real human
beings created in the image of God.

Your grandmother,

Bathsheba

Ten

Letter from Jezebel to her daughter

Based on 1 Kings 16:29-34; 18; 19; 21
        2 Kings 9; 11:1-4 (NEB)

Date: 870 B.C.

Jezebel and her daughter Athaliah had sons who were kings and allies. Both kings had just been killed in battle by Jehu, a commander who betrayed them because the Hebrew prophet had anointed him to be the next king of Israel.

Dear Athaliah,

The sounds of the bloody battle have ceased. My servant has brought word to me that our sons are dead: a King of Israel and a King of Judah both slain by Jehu the traitor. Jehu is on his way here to Jezreel. Execution is my certain fate.

I know how a queen faces death. I have painted my eyes and dressed my hair. My courage is bolstered. Jehu will find me in my palace.

It is not my death that I wonder about but my life. I want my years in this world to have made a difference. I want to be remembered as a woman who accepted the duties required of a daughter of a great king. I did not find it a pleasant duty when my marriage was arranged with Ahab, King of Israel, but I knew my father was forming various alliances as

buffers against the growing aggressiveness of Assyria. A
royal marriage has always been a useful tool and I was
prepared to be a queen to King Ahab.

Of even greater importance to me than my duties as a
daughter and a queen, however, were my religious respon-
sibilities as a priestess of the Great Goddess Ashtarath and
her consort Baal. I had heard that in Israel there existed a
cult worshiping one God, whose name was Yahweh. My
father told me that although in earlier generations the
Jewish kings had been faithful to Yahweh, it was no longer
so. In fact, he assured me I would find the worship of
Ashtarath and Baal flourishing. He allowed me, however,
to take hundreds of my own priests with me in order to
ensure that our beliefs were presented properly.

So I arrived in Israel and was married to Ahab. He was a
disappointment to me. He was a man with no real religious
commitment. He would seem to worship the Queen of
Heaven, but on occasion he would pay lip service to Yahweh.
He was often influenced by a militant, evil-tempered old
man named Elijah, who claimed to be Yahweh's prophet.

Not only was Ahab indecisive in religious matters, but he
did not understand how to be a strong king. The incident
involving Naboth's vineyard occurred early in our marriage.
Ahab asked the farmer Naboth to sell him a vineyard that
was near the palace. When the man refused, Ahab went
home, lay down on his bed, covered his face, and refused to
eat! I found him so and I could not believe I was beholding
a king, pouting and sullen because a simple peasant would
not agree to sell a vineyard.

I suggested to him how a king should handle a peasant.
The stories told about me by the Yahweh-worshiping
Israelites say that I carried out the plan that resulted in
Naboth's death. My husband was indeed unimaginative,
but he did not object to carrying out such a plan himself. It
was his name and his seal on the order to falsely accuse the

farmer; it was the elders and notables of Naboth's own city who chose to accept the accusations. When I heard of Naboth's death, I told Ahab now he could take possession of the vineyard. Even in the stories the Israelites tell, Ahab is described as showing no surprise nor asking for any details. That is not the picture of an innocent man with a conniving wife. He was delighted with his new possession until Elijah frightened him with curses and threats. Again Ahab forgot he was a king and tore his clothes, put on sack cloth, and went about muttering to himself.

I realized I could not count on Ahab to protect my priests and my temple of the Great Goddess Ashtarath. Ahab himself arranged the infamous ambush on Mount Carmel where over eight hundred of my priests were murdered. Perhaps because of agreements with my father or because of his own spiritual conflicts, Ahab did not ever completely align himself with Elijah. I think he got a perverted pleasure from watching the priest of Yahweh confront my priests.

After Ahab's death your older brother reigned in Israel and was later succeeded by your second brother. The nation continued to recognize the Great Goddess as supreme. The Yahweh-worshipers and their prophets, first Elijah, then Elisha, battled me, the chief priestess of Ashtarath, whenever possible. They were fanatically determined to destroy our religion.

All in all those were good years for us. You had married the King of Judah and you were as devout a priestess of Ashtarath as I. So for a long time most of the people of Israel and Judah revered our Goddess. This worship continued after your son became King of Judah.

But the good years are gone here, Athaliah. I know that after Jehu murders me, he will try to wipe out my temples and all traces of my religion. With my letter as forewarning perhaps you will be able to seize your dead son's throne in Judah, and, thus, continue to serve our Goddess.

So I will die for my beliefs. Have I been wrong? One must ask this question at the end of life. There was a time when I wanted to know about the God Yahweh. In some of the Hebrew writings I glimpsed a picture of an unusual Creator, one who not only judges, but loves and forgives, one who wants not murder in his name but a life of service. One writer said that the human being was created in the image of this God to glorify not himself but God. When I first heard Israelites speak of the One God, I felt a yearning in my heart that this might be a god who *was one*, maleness and femaleness together in complete deity as an example for complete humanity.

As I studied the Mosaic laws, however, I came to realize that Yahweh is understood as a male god whose laws are designed to promote men's welfare. Women are considered men's property. A law affecting a woman has as its purpose the economic and sexual welfare of the man who owns her. A man has sexual freedom as long as he does not infringe on another man's wife, virgin daughter, or maidservant (Deuteronomy 5:21). It is only a woman, not a man, who is stoned to death for losing virginity before marriage (Deuteronomy 22:13-21). Property rights are inherited through the males. Names are passed on through males. Daughters are not worth much. I recall one writing in which a man offers his virgin daughters to some invaders of his home if they will agree not to take his male guests in a homosexual rape (Genesis 19:5-8).

How could I turn from my Goddess, the Queen of Heaven, and worship Yahweh who only protects men? My beliefs grow out of religious tradition rooted in a profound respect for woman's ability to create life. When men realized that they, too, had a part in the birth of a child, they developed the idea of a sexual morality, but only for women. These morality laws, that they said came from their god, seemed peculiarly designed to ensure knowledge of a man's paternity.

At this point I cannot choose Yahweh over Ashtarath. To worship him would be to deny woman's equality with man. Perhaps Yahweh is the One God who created us all, but the prophet who can describe him fully has not yet been sent to humankind.

Athaliah, I hear chariot wheels rolling over the stones of my courtyard. Jehu is here. I know he comes to carry out the order of his priest Elijah to kill me and destroy my body so no one can even pay honor to me in death and say, "Here lies Jezebel." But, Athaliah, my daughter, if my servant succeeds in bringing this letter to you, consider my soul's searching for truth and say, "*This* was Jezebel."

Signed,

Your mother
On earth, Queen of Israel
In Heaven, daughter of Ashtarath

Eleven

Letter from Mary to her cousin

Based on Mark, Luke, and John (NEB)

Date: A day after the crucifixion. 33 A.D.

> When they saw him, they recounted what they had been told about this child; and all who heard were astonished at what the shepherds said. But Mary treasured up all these things and pondered over them.
>
> Luke 2:17-19

> As they could not find him they returned to Jerusalem to look for him; and after three days they found him sitting in the temple surrounded by the teachers, listening to them and putting questions; and all who heard him were amazed at his intelligence and the answers he gave. His parents were astonished to see him there, and his mother said to him. "My son, why have you treated us like this? Your father and I have been searching for you in great anxiety." "What made you search?" he said. "Did you not know that I was bound to be in my Father's house?" But they did not understand what he meant. Then he went back with them to Nazareth, and continued to be under their authority; his mother treasured up all these things in her heart.
>
> Luke 2:45-52

Dear Elizabeth,

Jesus died yesterday. You have been aware of each step my son took toward his cross, so I write these words not to inform you of his death but rather as a preface to what I must put down about his life. I came to visit you when I first knew I was to bear this son; I again need to share my deepest thoughts with you, dear friend and cousin.

After Jesus's body was taken down from the cross, his disciple John begged me not to return to my house alone. But I wanted time to think and to write to you.

There are those who say Jesus was not a good son. Although he spent his childhood learning the carpenter's trade, it was obvious he did not intend to center his life on this work. The year he was twelve Joseph and I had made our usual pilgrimage to Jerusalem for the Passover festival. Realizing that Jesus was not with the group on the way home, we returned to the city to look for him. After three days we found him sitting in the temple surrounded by the teachers, listening to them and questioning them. I said, "My son, why have you treated us like this? Your father and I have been searching for you in great anxiety." "What made you search?" he said. "Did you not know that I was bound to be in my Father's house?" (Luke 2:41-51).

I realized then that Jesus was already independent of me as a mother. But he returned home with us and continued working in the shop. I treasured his presence, but I kept the uneasy sense that I had already lost a son. I was haunted by the words the old man Simeon had spoken at Jesus's circumcision: "This child is destined to be a sign which men reject; and you too shall be pierced to the heart" (Luke 2:34-35).

When Jesus finally gave up the steady income from carpentry and became a wandering preacher, my friends grieved for me. My husband had died and now my eldest son seemed disinterested in providing financially for me.

I recall the time Jesus's brothers and I went to fetch him from a house in the hill-country. We thought he needed protection from people who were accusing him of madness.

Because of the crowds we were unable to enter the house, so we sent a message in asking him to come out. The report came back that Jesus had looked around at those sitting in the circle about him and had said, "Who is my mother? Who are my brothers? *Here* are my mother and my brothers. Whoever does the will of God is my brother, my sister, my mother" (Mark 3:31-35).

Then my friends pitied me more and said my son had turned his back on me. I knew better than this. He was saying something important to all of us, and especially to me, a woman. He had reserved the word *father* to define his relationship to God. All other believers were equal with Jesus in value! I was worthwhile, not because I gave birth to a particular man-child, but because I did the will of God.

Another time a voice from the crowd around Jesus called out, "Happy the womb that carried you and the breasts that suckled you!" Again Jesus rejected the idea that my life's only meaning lay in producing a noted son. He responded, "No, happy are those who hear the word of God and keep it" (Luke 11:27-28). He made me responsible for myself; he showed me the way to fulfill my potential. We stood as brother and sister before God our Father!

Elizabeth, do you understand that not only my son died yesterday, but a brother who loved me beyond any other love I have known? He was able to love all people whose lives touched his, yet I never felt he took from me to give to another. How I will miss him. I will struggle to hold on to the selfhood he gave me.

Jesus knew it would not be easy for me, a woman, to keep this new feeling of equality and worth. In his last moments of life he thought about my special need. Even in the indescribable agony that crucifixion brings, he was able to speak to me and to John standing near the cross. "Mother, there is your son," he whispered. And to John, "There is your mother" (John 19:25-27).

There are those who question why I was removed from the charge of James, my second son. But Jesus knew his brother well. James has always followed the Jewish law rigidly (Galatians 2:12; Acts 21:18-26). It must have been hard for him to accept the illegality of Jesus' birth; perhaps he never has seen Jesus as a lawful brother or me as a chaste woman. Did Jesus suspect James would not respect me as a person, that he would undermine my new sense of worth? Jesus offered me and the disciple he loved to each other in an equal relationship. John's capacity for understanding this was much greater than James'. John had heard and believed Jesus' prayer:

> The glory which thou gavest me I have given to them, that they may be one, as we are one; I in them and thou in me, may they be perfectly one.
>
> John 17:22-23

I will miss Jesus very much. Do you remember, Elizabeth, what I said to you when I visited you over thirty years ago:

> so wonderfully has he dealt with me,
>   the Lord, the Mighty One. . .
> he has brought down monarchs from their thrones
>   but the humble have been lifted high.
>
> Luke 1:49, 52

Now I understand my own words; I have truly been lifted high!

Your cousin,

Mary

Twelve

Letter from Martha to her sister

Based on Luke 10:38-42 and John 11; 12:1-3 (NEB)

Date: About 36 A.D.

> While they were on their way Jesus came to a village where a woman named Martha made him welcome in her home. She had a sister, Mary, who seated herself at the Lord's feet and stayed there listening to his words. Now Martha was distracted by her many tasks, so she came to him and said, 'Lord, do you not care that my sister has left me to get on with the work by myself? Tell her to come and lend a hand.' But the Lord answered, 'Martha, Martha, you are fretting and fussing about so many things; but one thing is necessary. The part that Mary has chosen is best; and it shall not be taken away from her.'
>
> Luke 10:38-42

Dear Mary,

Only a few months ago I left Bethany to live in the Jerusalem Christian community. It has been exciting to be part of the spreading of the gospel. How grateful I am that you insisted I go on this mission. I want nothing more than to tell people about our Lord and what he taught us.

I have been surprised to find that you and I are both well known because our story is told wherever the gospel is preached. Remember the time Jesus was visiting with us and I became annoyed because you were not helping prepare the meal? Jesus said to me:

> Martha, Martha, you are fretting and fussing about so many things, but one thing is necessary. The part Mary has chosen is best; and it shall not be taken from her.
>
> Luke 10:40-42

Some of the people hearing this story ask if Jesus was saying housework is not important. I remind them that Jesus made no comment on the value of different kinds of work. He only said that listening to his teachings is the "best part". I explain to my audience that if we can understand what Jesus said, the problem of who performs a particular job will disappear. Furthermore, we women must take on the responsibility of interpreting Jesus's words for ourselves.

I did not have to be told this twice! The very next time you and I saw our Lord it was I who left you tending the house and went out to meet Jesus. Lazarus had died and I spoke accusingly:

> "If you had been here, sir, my brother would not have died. Even now I know that whatever you ask of God, God will grant you."
>
> Jesus said, "Your brother will rise again." "I know he will rise again," I said, "at the resurrection on the last day."
>
> Jesus said, "I am the resurrection and I am life. If a man has faith in me, even though he die, he shall come to life; and no one who is alive and has faith shall ever die. Do you believe this?"

I listened to Jesus myself. I chose the best part. I made my independent statement of faith: "Lord, I do; I now believe that you are the Messiah, the Son of God who was to come into the world" (John 11).

Remember, I came back to the house and told you Jesus was asking for you. Tears come in my eyes even as I write those dear words, "Jesus was asking for you," for I knew then as I know now the special feeling Jesus had for you and you for him. He suffered with and for all of us, but you and he wept together, you for Lazarus and he for you. He knew what pain you had yet to bear, and the raising of Lazarus would only bring it closer.

After this mighty act, Jesus no longer went about publicly but went to Ephraim for a while with some friends. Six days before the Passover festival he came back to our home. We had a supper in honor of Lazarus. Again I served the food, but this time there was no resentment in my heart. My identity was secure. Serving my Lord's supper was an honor for any woman or man.

After supper you went out of the room and returned with the precious oil of nard that had been put away for your own burial. You anointed the feet of Jesus and wiped them with your hair. The fragrance filled the house (John 12:1-3).

Mary, had you, above all the disciples, heard Jesus's words so well that you realized he was preparing to die? Did you anoint him to show him you understood? I had repeated to you the words he had said to me: "no one who is alive and has faith shall ever die." Was it your faith that let you anoint him for burial so lovingly and place your hope in his return?

As I am called to witness here in Jerusalem to our Risen Lord, I find I am looking at these past incidents and asking myself questions. You recognized complete humanity in Jesus. I saw that he was God. Where do our understandings meet? Write to me, Mary; I am hungry for new insight.

Your loving sister,

Martha

Thirteen

Letter from Mary of Magdala

Based on Mark 5:25-34; 16:9-11; Luke 8:1-2; John 20;
Philippians 4:15; Acts 16:11-15 (NEB)

Date: About 52 A.D.

> So we sailed from Troas and made a straight run to Samo-
> thrace, the next day to Neapolis, and from there to Philippi,
> a city of the first rank in that district of Macedonia, and a
> Roman colony. Here we stayed for some days, and on the
> Sabbath day we went outside the city gate by the riverside,
> where we thought there would be a place of prayer, and sat
> down and talked to the women who had gathered there. One
> of them named Lydia, a dealer in purple fabric from the city
> of Thyatira, who was a worshipper of God, was listening,
> and the Lord opened her heart to respond to what Paul said.
> She was baptized, and her household with her, and then she
> said to us, 'If you have judged me to be a believer in the
> Lord, I beg you to come and stay in my house.' And she
> insisted on our going.
>
> Acts 16:11-15

Dear Lydia,

I received word from Paul of your baptism. He often asks
one of us disciples who was a friend of Jesus to write a new
convert about her experience. As the faith grows, surely we

will have to put these experiences in book form. But I never tire of telling about my Lord.

I was born and raised in Magdala, a Galilean city wealthy through commerce and industry. Most of the population is Gentile and there are of course pagan religious practices. The town has a bad reputation in the eyes of the Jews. Regardless, my family's livelihood required our living there.

It was not easy to grow up part of a minority, especially one whose religion kept its members from participating in most of the city's activities. As a young girl I always felt mixed up and anxious with a deep unexplainable fear. My early life blurs in my memory; I know my family and the church leaders said I was possessed of seven devils. When my parents heard of the Jewish healer who was performing miracles near Jerusalem, they took me to him. As far as I am concerned my life really began when Jesus touched me and made me whole (Luke 8:1-2). From then on I wanted only to travel with him and serve him. In gratitude my parents provided a small income for me and I was free to do as I wished. I have chosen to forego marriage and dedicate myself to the Lord's business. This is an alternative Jesus Christ has given me.

In a letter I must be brief, but I would like to tell you about another woman who, like me, was healed by Jesus. We never found out her name so we call her the Woman with the Hemorrhage (Mark 5:25-34). She had suffered for twelve years with this physically debilitating and personally embarrassing condition. She was considered unclean and could not participate in any religious ceremony. The mysterious connection between woman's blood and the creation of life frightened Jewish men and had to be attacked by laws that called her unclean and therefore unholy. Even though you are Gentile, Lydia, you probably have observed similar processes in other male-dominated religions.

Thinking a Jewish man would be bound by law to avoid any contact with her, the woman was afraid to ask Jesus to touch her. In secrecy and shame she reached out and put her hand on his cloak. Instantly she knew she was cured! At the same time Jesus, aware that power had gone out of him, turned in the crowd and asked, "Who touched me?"

How typical of our Lord this was! He knew she had been physically healed yet he insisted she identify herself. He wanted her to confront him and to know he was not offended by her act. She received a second healing! No longer was a physical condition, an issue of blood, to be considered unclean. She had been freed from superstition and prejudice and allowed to touch the Christ. What greater religious ceremony could there be!

I could tell you many other stories about Jesus but I must get to the most important fact, his resurrection!

Early on Sunday morning while it was still dark I came to the cave where he had been laid. Seeing the stone had been removed from the opening, I ran to Peter and John and cried, "They have taken the Lord out of his tomb!" They rushed to the tomb, went inside, and saw that Jesus's body was indeed gone. The two men went home but I stood outside the tomb weeping. Suddenly I saw a man standing there. "Why are you weeping? Who is it you are looking for?" he asked. Thinking it was the gardener, I answered, "If it is you, sir, who removed him, tell me where you have laid him, and I will take him away." The man said my name, "Mary!" and I recognized him as my Master! He would not let me touch him but told me to go and tell the other disciples he lived (John 20).

I carried the good news to the others. In their sorrow they did not believe me. Later when they, too, saw him, he reproached them for their disbelief (Mark 16:9-15). How grateful I am that I knew him when he called my name. He does live, Lydia! I have seen the Risen Lord!

I know you understand the excitement that comes in preaching the good news. Paul wrote that not only did you lead your whole household to Christ, but your home is used as a meeting place (Acts 16:14-15). From his letter I sense a special commitment in the believers of Philippi (Philippians 4:15). All of us thank God for your leadership.

Your sister in Christ,

Mary of Magdala

Fourteen

Letter from Priscilla

Based on Acts 18:1-3, 24-26; other references indicated in letter (NEB)

Date: About 60 A.D.

> I appeal to you, my brothers, in the name of our Lord Jesus Christ: agree among yourselves, and avoid divisions; be firmly joined in unity of mind and thought. I have been told, my brothers, by Chloe's people that there are quarrels among you. What I mean is this: each of you is saying, 'I am Paul's man', or 'I am for Apollos'; 'I follow Cephas', or 'I am Christ's.'
>
> 1 Corinthians 1:10-12

Dear Daughter,

You are right to be concerned over the doctrinal arguing going on within your Christian community. You are also justified in your fear that our Lord's teaching of the equality of men and women may be compromised. With no generally accepted written document to guide us, we Christians are being influenced by our local preacher's interpretations of various existing fragments of Christian writings. The time is coming soon when we must gather this material together, study it, and preserve that which most truly reflects the mind of our Lord. I hope and pray his liberating attitude toward women will shine forth clearly in all writings we mark for future generations.

From the accounts of eyewitnesses it is clear that Jesus himself had confidence in women's ability to understand and to preach his message. Through God's grace it was two women who first realized Jesus was sent for all people. Do you recall the Canaanite woman who insisted Jesus cure her daughter? Although discouraged by the apostles around Jesus, she saw within our Lord something more than a Messiah to Israel (Matthew 15:21-28).

The other woman I speak of was a Samaritan, called unclean by the Jews. When the disciples found Jesus talking to her, they were astonished, but none of them even asked, "Why are you talking to her?" They could not have imagined that in their absence, Jesus had revealed to this foreign woman that he was indeed the Messiah, *her* Messiah! This woman, chosen by Jesus himself as a witness, went into her village with the news. Many Samaritans came to believe in him because of her testimony (John 4:8-42).

From the accounts of Jesus' mother Mary, Mary and Martha of Bethany, and Mary of Magdala we know that for Jesus a woman's value lay not in her relationship to a certain father, husband, or son. He never implied that every woman should marry, but if she did, he said the marriage vows were the same for both husband and wife (Mark 10:2-12).

Your father Aquila and I have enjoyed a Christian marriage for many years. Equal in our Lord's sight, we have lived and loved together, worked together at our trade, witnessed enthusiastically for our Saviour. We have gone through persecution and exile together, but also together we have found our eternal home in Jesus the Christ. We praise God!

You have written me that in your congregation you have heard words purported to be those of our dear friend and fellow believer, Paul, words that seem to be against women's self-expression or leadership in the church or at home (1

Corinthians 11:3-9; 14:33-35; Ephesians 5:22-24). This is hard for me to believe.

For eighteen months Paul lived with Aquila and me. We had many discussions about the faith (Acts 18:1-3). Often he said that in Christ there is no such thing as male or female (Galatians 3:28-29). He actually believes our Lord can best be served by one who chooses the single life. This applies to both men and women (1 Corinthians 7:32-34). However, to those who decide to marry, Paul echoes Jesus' message closely. He teaches a single standard regarding sexual relations in and out of marriage, and a divorce law that, while very strict, is the same for the husband as for the wife (1 Corinthians 7:1-11).

Paul believes that women can prophesy (1 Corinthians 11:5; Acts 21:9), therefore it is hard to believe he would say they cannot speak in church! And how could he demand the celibate woman "ask her husband"? If Paul says women should keep their place, what place could that be? Lydia and I are happy working at professions. Phoebe holds a church office in Cenchreae and on occasion carries a letter from Paul to Rome (Romans 16:1-2). Junia, whom Paul calls an apostle (as he does himself), has witnessed to her Lord in prison (Romans 16:6-7; 1 Corinthians 9:1). Dorcas, a disciple, fills her days with sewing for the poor (Acts 9:36). Nympha (Colossians 4:15) and Mary and Martha offer their homes as churches. Mary of Magdala has traveled about the country following our Lord.

The words you are being told were Paul's may have been added to his letter by someone else. A believer, anxious to prove a point about his favorite preacher—Apollos, Peter, or Paul—might even write a whole letter and sign it with his favorite's name. I can even face the possibility that my friend Paul did indeed write contradictory opinions. He is, after all, a human, and subject to the pressures of the culture we live in. Remember the apostle Peter went back on his

word more than once (Galatians 2:11-21). We have not
taken his mistakes as models for our lives, nor have we
denied all that was good in him. So be it for Paul.

Our ancient scriptures tell us about women who died in
faith.

> And what is faith? Faith gives substance to our hopes, and
> makes us certain of realities we do not see. . . . They were
> not yet in possession of the things promised but had seen
> them far ahead and hailed them.
>
> Hebrews 11:1, 13

Dear daughter, the reality is here. It is that men and
women were both created in God's image. Side by side we
must struggle to care for our world: the people in it, even
the fish, the birds, the wild animals, the reptiles, the plants
that bear seed, the waters and the dry land (Genesis 1). Side
by side we exit to eternity secure in the love of Jesus Christ.

Your mother,

Priscilla

Questions for Discussion

One: Dear Daughter

(Letter from Eve)

Based on Genesis 2:5-5:5 (New English Bible)

1. Does knowing good from evil lead to death? (What is death?)

2. If there were no evil, could there be good?

3. Can we make another person's choices? What is our obligation to another person? Do you think Eve made Adam's choice for him?

4. Is it part of man's nature to succumb to the temptation of woman?

5. In Genesis 3:16 part of woman's punishment was to have sexual desire for her husband and as a result be dominated by him. Was man to be punished for having sexual desire for his wife?

6. Is pain in childbearing still considered part of woman's punishment for her sexual desire?

7. If a "bad" woman tempts a man and causes him to sin, is the converse true that "the love of a good woman" can save a man? Has man expected woman to redeem him? Are women expected to see to the religious training of the children?

8. What is the effect on a human if he/she cannot blame someone else for his/her sin? Consider conflicts between races, religions, sexes, classes, nations, generations.

Two: Dear Milcah

(Letter from Sarah)

Based on Genesis 11:27-13:18; 15:1-5; 16; 17; 18; 21; 22 (NEB)

1. Did Sarah commit adultery by going into Pharaoh's harem?

2. What was Pharaoh's offense?

3. In Genesis 16:7-12 the angel of the Lord speaks directly to Hagar concerning her descendants. Why doesn't the Lord communicate directly with Sarah?

4. In Genesis 18:1-15, the passage in which a son is predicted for Sarah, do you think Abraham and Sarah recognize the strangers as God's messengers? What does Sarah's laughter suggest about her relationship with God?

5. In Genesis 18:20-33 Abraham argues with God over God's decision to wipe out Sodom and Gomorrah. Why doesn't Abraham argue with God over the sacrifice of Isaac?

6. Why doesn't Abraham offer himself as a sacrifice in place of Isaac?

7. How do you think God speaks to us through other people?

Three: Dear Grandmother

(Letter from Rebecca)

Based on Genesis 24:1-67; 25; 26; 27; 28:1-9 (NEB)

1. Did Rebecca play an active role in her selection by Abraham's servant? What does the writer of Genesis imply (Genesis 24:14)?

2. Why would the servant bargain with God over how to select Isaac's wife? Do we ever attempt this same sort of thing with God? Why?

3. When asked whose daughter she was, how did Rebecca identify herself (Genesis 24:45)? Why did she mention her grandmother but not her mother?

4. Why do you think Rebecca agreed to go with Abraham's servant?

5. In the blessing given Rebecca by her family (Genesis 24:60) what is revealed about the role of men and women?

6. Was Rebecca wrong to help in tricking Isaac? Do you think the writer of Genesis thinks she was wrong?

7. When Isaac realized he had been deceived, why couldn't he correct his error? Why wasn't he angry with Rebecca?

8. Why do you think God is described as speaking directly to Rebecca (Genesis 25:23)?

9. Even today parents may show partiality to one child. Compare the ancient and modern family's attitude.

Four: Dearest Dinah

(Letter from Leah)

Based on Genesis 29: 30:14-26; 32; 33; 34

1. Both Rebecca and Rachel were chosen as wives at first sight. What does this imply about women's role at that time? Today how are women chosen to be wives?

2. In Genesis 30:1-13 both Rachel and Leah willingly offer their slave-girls to Jacob. Why do they do this? Is this idea reflected in our tradition of children's carrying only their father's name? The writer has Leah say, "God has rewarded me because I gave my slave-girl to my husband." What does this suggest about the beliefs of the time?

4. What sort of person does Esau seem to be? Do you think God could have worked through him as easily as through Jacob? If so why didn't he?

5. Why do you think Jacob asked to be buried beside Leah (Genesis 49:29-32)?

6. Leah had a son Judah from whom Jesus was descended (Matthew 1:1-16). Does this have any implication as to Leah's relationship with God?

7. Both Dinah and Leah apparently engaged in premarital sex. What was the difference from the family point of view? Do you believe a woman is dishonored by rape? If men and women were equally vulnerable to rape, do you think a man and a woman would react in the same way to the rape of his/her spouse? How do our beliefs in Christ apply here?

7. A common biblical symbol of Israel falling away from God is the woman who is unfaithful to her husband. Why is the same point never illustrated by a man's unfaithfulness to his wife?

Five: Dear Deborah

(Letter from Jael)

Based on Judges 4 and 5 (NEB)

1. It was not customary to have a female judge. What might have led to Deborah's becoming one?

2. Why did Barak insist on Deborah's going with him into battle? What if the battle had failed?

3. Do you think one should be able to put a belief into action? For example: If you believe in capital punishment, could you pull the switch and watch the death? If you do not believe in it, can you pay the taxes necessary to run humane prisons with enough staff to protect society from criminals? If you believe in abortion, could you perform the abortion? If you do not believe in it, can you accept your share of the responsibility for unwanted children, who may be abused emotionally and physically?

4. How did Deborah feel about Jael (Judges 5:24-27)? How do you feel about her?

5. What does loyalty to one's husband or wife mean to you? Do you think Jael was disloyal?

6. Would you be reluctant to have a woman priest or minister? What would you see as advantages and disadvantages?

Six: To the Wife of Manoah
(Letter from Delilah)

Based on Judges 13; 14; 15; 16 (NEB)

1. Why did the Israelites equate both defeat and victory in battle as "judgment" from God? Do you think they believed there was only one God over the world?

2. What sort of personality did God seem to have in the ancient Hebrew mind? Was there anything unique about the understanding the Israelites had of God?

3. What was Samson's attitude toward women? Can you identify with Delilah? Are there situations today in which a woman can find no protection from an irate suitor or husband?

4. What role did Samson play in his consecration to God?

5. Samson was a hero. Was he worthy of the people's adulation? When you hear the word "hero" or "heroine" today, what sort of person comes to mind?

6. How have Samson and Delilah been presented in traditional Bible stories read to children? What might a child have been expected to learn from such a story?

Seven: Dear Orpah
(Letter from Ruth)

Based on The Book of Ruth (NEB)

1. Why did Naomi change her mind about taking Ruth and Orpah with her?

2. Naomi tells Ruth to go back to her people and her gods. What does this imply about Naomi's concept of Yahweh?

3. Why does the writer repeatedly mention that Ruth is a Moabite?

4. What picture of Ruth do you get from the Bible story?

5. What sort of man was Boaz? Is he the hero of the story?

6. Was Naomi wrong to scheme to get Boaz to marry Ruth? How would you feel about similar scheming today? Compare the trick played on Boaz with the one Leah's father played on Jacob.

7. Why was it important that Ruth have a son (Ruth 4:10)?

8. Why do you think Ruth's famous statement of loyalty to Naomi has been taken out of context and used in modern times as a wedding song?

9. Note the mention of Tamar in Ruth 4:12. In the Matthew 1:1-16 genealogy of Jesus three women other than Mary are mentioned by name: Tamar, Rahab, and Ruth. What explanation might there be for this (Genesis 38:6-29) (Joshua 2:1-24)?

Eight: Dear Merab

(Letter from Michal)

Based on 1 Samuel 18:10-30; 19:1-17; 25:1-44
2 Samuel 3:2-5; 5; 6; 21; 22; 23 (NEB)

1. Besides Bible stories we all read fairy stories in which the king gave "the princess and half the kingdom" to the hero. Why didn't this seem dehumanizing to the young female reader?

2. Some Christian marriage services ask "Who gives this woman?" What is the implication?

3. Why did Saul offer first Merab, than Michal to David? Why did David accept? How did Saul feel about Michal's being in love with David (1 Samuel 18:10-29)?

4. Why did Michal keep "household gods" (1 Samuel 19:12)?

5. Why did the author of the Scriptures include the lines about Michal's husband Palti's weeping for her (2 Samuel 4:16)?

6. Did David, Michal, and Palti have alternative ways to behave?

7. Why did Michal berate David for dancing scantily clad in the streets? Why did David do so? Does the Bible writer think David was right?

8. In this letter Michal wonders why a man's attitude toward women is not a test of his character. Do you think this was true then? What about the present time? Consider the old expression: "All's fair in love and war."

Nine: Dear Taphath

(Letter from Bathsheba)

Based on 1 Kings 4:11; 2 Samuel 11:1-27; 12:1-25 (NEB)

1. In 2 Samuel 12:7-9 Nathan says to David: "This is the word of the Lord the God of Israel to you, 'I anointed you king over Israel, I rescued you from the power of Saul, I gave you your master's daughter and his wives to be your own, I gave you the daughters of Israel and Judah; and, had this not been enough, I would have added other favors as great. Why then have you flouted the word of the Lord by doing what is wrong in my eyes?' "
What does this say about women's position? Do you believe this was the word of God? By what standard could David evaluate the prophet's message? What is the relationship between God and David? Between God and Nathan? What would a woman feel about her relationship to a God who spoke this way?

2. Do you think David loved Bathsheba?

3. Which would have been the better life: wife of Uriah or wife of David?

4. Matthew 1:1-16 says "wife of Uriah" was an ancestor of Jesus. Why is she not called by name? What is the significance of her kinship to Jesus?

Ten: Dear Athaliah

(Letter from Jezebel)

Based on 1 Kings 16:29-34; 18; 19; 21
2 Kings 9; 11:1-4 (NEB)

1. Why was Ahab reluctant to seize Naboth's vineyard (1 Kings 21:1-14)?

2. What was the accusation against Naboth (1 Kings 21:1-14)?

3. In 1 King 21:25-26 the writer declares Ahab's sins were "all at the prompting of Jezebel his wife." What concept of women is operative here?

4. Ahab indicated repentance by publicly rending his clothes, wearing sackcloth, and fasting. Why do you think Elijah believed this satisfied the Lord (1 Kings 21:27-29)?

5. Jezebel has been described as a "painted hussy." Do you think this is a fair description?

6. The followers of Ashtarath and of Yahweh wanted to destroy each other. As Christians what are our obligations to people of another religion?

7. If we wanted to elect a leader who was a faithful member of a certain religion or denomination, how would we ascertain this? By what the person said? By a report from his/her minister? Then would the minister become a prophet in the Old Testament sense? For many years a Roman Catholic had trouble winning a national election. Why? What are some of the abuses that can develop from allowing church and state to intertwine?

Eleven: Dear Elizabeth
(Letter from Mary)

Based on Mark, Luke, and John (NEB)

1. In what way can the human relationship between Mary and Jesus be a model for today's mother and child?

2. In 1 Timothy 2:15 the writer states that woman will be saved by motherhood. Does this idea reflect the teachings of Jesus?

3. Does the role a religious tradition gives to Mary relate to that tradition's attitude toward the ordinary woman?

4. Is the oppressed person more sensitive to the teachings of Jesus?

5. Compare Eve and Mary.

Twelve: Dear Mary
(Letter from Martha)

Based on Luke 10:38-42 and John 11; 12:1-3 (NEB)

1. Jesus did not place values on different kinds of work. Has the church followed him in this? Consider the paid and volunteer services a church requires. How has woman's role in the church been defined?

2. Who has traditionally interpreted Jesus's words for women? Why?

3. Why are there no recorded conversations between Jesus and Lazarus?

4. Why is Martha's statement of faith made before the raising of Lazarus?

5. Do you think it is significant that both Mary and Martha went out to meet Jesus? Also, that they went separately?

Thirteen: Dear Lydia

(Letter from Mary of Magdala)

Based on Mark 5:25-34; 16:9-11; Luke 8:1-2; John 20; Philippians 4:15; Acts 16:11-15 (NEB)

1. The Bible passages that mention Mary of Magdala are:

   Matthew 27:55; 28:1-10
   Mark 15:40; 16:1-9
   Luke 8:1-3; 24:1-12
   John 19:25; 20:1-18

   Tradition has called her a prostitute. Do you see any justification for this?

2. Do you think religious tradition has suggested a woman's sin is more likely to be of a sexual nature than is a man's? Why?

3. What role does the single woman have in the contemporary church?

4. What was the significance of Mary's inability to recognize the Lord until he called her by name?

5. Why did the Lord appear first to Mary if he knew her testimony would not be believed?

6. Why do you think Jesus insisted on the Woman with the Hemorrhage identifying herself?

7. Do you think women are still suspect because of their monthly cycle?

8. What kind of woman does Lydia seem to be? Do you think she has a husband (Acts 16:11-15)?

Fourteen: Dear Daughter

(Letter from Priscilla)

Based on Acts 18:1-4, 24-26;
and references indicated in letter (NEB)

1. The Bible passages relevant here are:

Acts 18:1-4, 24-26
Romans 16:3-5
Corinth 16:19-20

What sort of woman does Priscilla seem to be? What was the relationship between Paul and Priscilla? Why do you suppose Priscilla and Aquila stayed in Ephesus and did not go on with Paul to Syria?

2. Why are no women named as authors of any of the Scriptures?

3. In Matthew 15:21-28 and John 4:8-42 contrast Jesus and his apostles in their attitudes to the women.

4. Why does Jesus not say much about family life?

5. Is the contemporary church responding to the needs of non-traditional families?

Bibliography

William P. Barker, *Women and the Liberator*, Fleming H. Revell, 1972.

Mary Daly, *Beyond God the Father*, Beacon Press, 1973.

Alicia Faxon, *Women and Jesus*, United Church Press, 1973.

Georgia Harkness, *Women in Church and Society*, Abingdon Press, 1972.

Norah Lofts, *Women in the Old Testament*, Macmillan Co., 1949.

Carol Ochs, *Behind the Sex of God*, Beacon Press, 1977.

Rosemary Ruether, ed., *Religion and Sexism, Images of Women in the Jewish and Christian Traditions*, Simon and Shuster, 1974.

Letty M. Russell, *Human Liberation in a Feminist Perspective —A Theology*, Westminster Press, 1974.

Merlin Stone, *When God Was A Woman*, Dial Press, 1976.